This book is a
special gift for:

_____

From: _____

Date: _____

To Greg, Eloise, Greta,
and Simon - my favorite
quaranteam.

What is Coronavirus?

Christine Borst, PhD, LMFT

What is Coronavirus?
By Christine Borst PhD
Layout by Daniel Traynor

AimHi Press
Orlando, Florida
AimHiPress.com
© 2020, Christine Borst

Names: Borst, Christine. | Traynor, Daniel, Layout.
Title: What is Coronavirus? / by Christine Borst PhD
Description: Orlando, FL | AimHi Press, 2020. | Summary: What is Coronavirus? explains what is happening with this pandemic in a clear and simple way that will give children the tools to talk about their fears and empower them to feel safe and secure.
Identifiers: Library of Congress Control Number: 2020938273 |
ISBN 978-1-945493-27-0 (paperback)
Subjects: CYAC: Family. | Coronavirus. |Covid. | Quarantine. | Mental health. |
Classification: LCC PZ7.1.B67 Wha 2020(print)
LC record available at https://lccn.loc.gov/2019940825

You may be hearing a lot about Coronavirus these days (it's sometimes called COVID-19 too).

This is not what Coronavirus actually looks like, but sometimes it's fun to be a little silly when things are so serious. Maybe after you finish reading this book you can draw how you imagine it!

Coronavirus is a virus, kind of like a cold or the flu, that makes people sick.

Many people who get Coronavirus will only feel a little sick, or not sick at all. Many people with Coronavirus will not even know they have it.

A small amount of people who get Coronavirus may get very, very sick.

3

Coronavirus can be spread if someone with it coughs or sneezes into the air near another person.

People can get Coronavirus no matter what they look like, what color skin they have, or where they live.

4

It can also spread if a sick person touches a surface (like door handles or playground equipment) and someone else touches it after them.

Doctors and scientists are learning more about how it spreads every day.

The good news? You don't need to worry about this! It is the job of the grown-ups in your life to take care of you, and they are doing everything they can to keep you and your family safe.

7

It probably feels a little strange not going
to school, stores, parks, and play dates.

Maybe the grown-ups in your life used to leave your house to go to work, and now they are doing work at home while you are there too.

It can be tough to stay home all of the time, and it's okay to feel grumpy or tired of being around your family, even though you love them.

Grown-ups might act a little cranky too.

If we all stay home, fewer
people will get the virus.

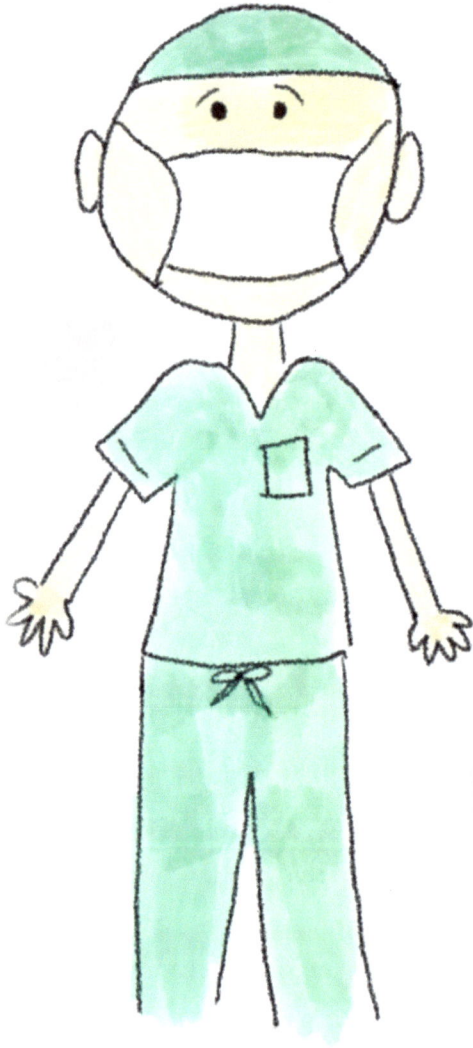

While we are at home, doctors, nurses, and other healthcare workers can work hard to get everyone healthy again!

There are many things you can do to help while the grown-ups are taking care of making the virus go away.

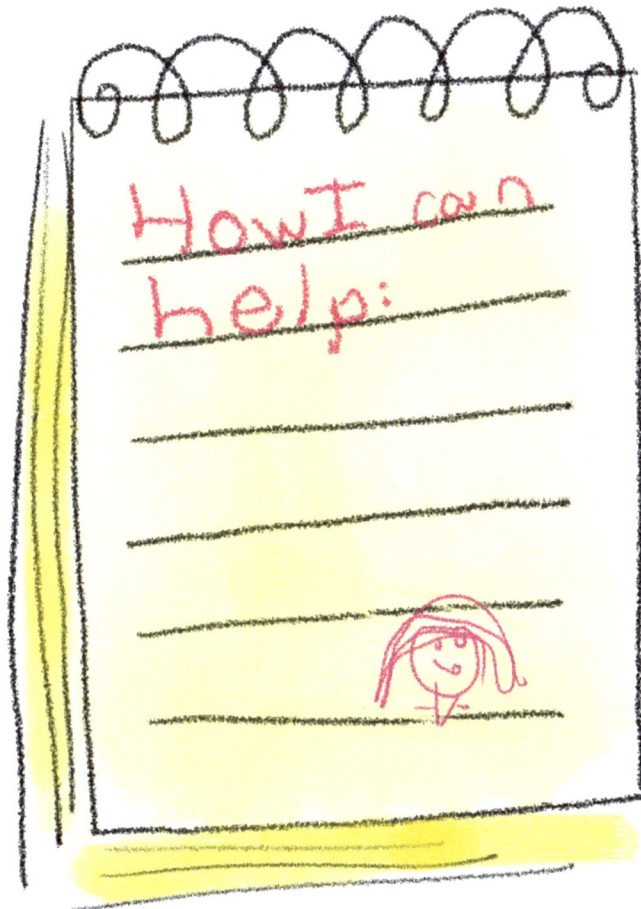

Wash your hands after you go to the bathroom, before you eat, if you cough or sneeze, and when you finish playing. Be sure to wash with soap for at least 20 seconds - that's long enough to sing Happy Birthday twice!

SOAP

Keep your body healthy by drinking lots of water, and eating a rainbow of foods (like fruits and veggies).

Be sure to get a good night's sleep!

If you can, get lots of sunshine and fresh air! Play in your yard (if you have one), sit on your porch, or even go for a walk, hike, or bike ride with your family.

17

Just remember to stay away from other people for now. If you see your neighbors, just smile and wave - this won't last forever!

Draw pictures and write notes for your family and friends - they will love getting mail!

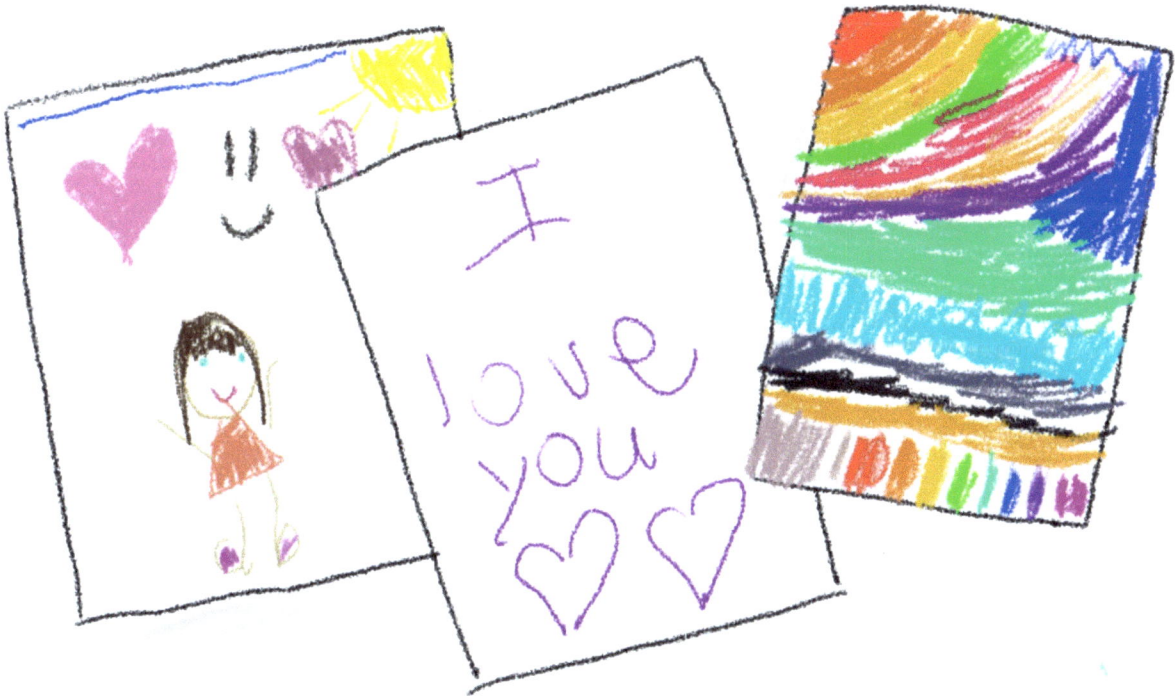

Do fun activities to move your body, even if you can't get outside! Turn on some music and have a dance party, or search the internet for kid yoga or kid exercise videos.

Call your friends,
grandparents, aunts, uncles,
and cousins to say hello!

This might feel like a weird and scary time, but there are also many wonderful things happening.

Today we are thankful for: 3/23
· Daddy's birthday!
· Facetiming with our grandparents
· Frozen II on Disney+
· Time together to make crafts
· The Sunshine!

Making a list of things you and your family are thankful for every day may help everyone feel a little better.

Nobody knows for sure how long this will last, so we will all have to be patient together. Remember, it's okay to feel sad, mad, or scared, and it's okay to ask questions, even if we don't know all of the answers right now.

No matter what, you are safe, and you are loved.

My Daily Journal

Things might feel scary right now, but one way that can help you feel better is to write (and draw!) your feelings. Start a Daily Journal by completing the following:

1. Ask an adult if you can get a notebook or write on the computer.
2. Write something each day in your journal.
   Start with how you're feeling that day, but then add something fun! You could:
   - Write down what you want to do that day
   - Draw a picture of what makes you happy
   - Write a poem or song
   - Make a list of movies and TV you want see or books you want to read
   - Write something nice about your family and friends
3. Share what you wrote. You could have a video call, write a letter or email, or talk to a family member.

Using your imagination can help this time go by quickly!
Having a journal can help you remember how much your friends and family care about you.

We are all in this together.

Dear Parents,

 Please know that you are doing an amazing job!

This isn't an easy time (understatement) and helping kids feel safe and secure is so important. Remember to take care of yourself so you can take care of others.

Thank you so much for your purchase – 100% of the profit from this book will go to helping families and small businesses impacted by COVID-19 and other pandemics.

Thanks for all that you do!

Christine

P.S. Big thanks to my 6 year old daughter Eloise for illustrating the child art throughout the book!

Christine Borst, PhD, LMFT

Dr. Christine Borst is a professor, licensed therapist, creative, mom of three, surgeon's wife, and happy Coloradan. She is co-founder of Lemon Rising, a community for inspiring authentic joy and health. Find her on Instagram at @christine_e_bee and @lemon.rising, and visit her website at christineborst.com to connect.

Visit AimHiPress.com for more books and other products from AimHi Press and the rest of the Newhouse Creative Group family!

Inspiring the readers and writers of today and tomorrow!

Newhouse Creative Group: Inspiring the Readers and Writers of Today and Tomorrow

www.ingramcontent.com/pod-product-compliance
Lightning Source LLC
Chambersburg PA
CBHW042107040426
42448CB00002B/175